Thank you for reading our Turkish Heritage Songbook. We created the Heritage Songbook Series to promote musical understanding between children, parents, and educators around the world.

We hope you spend many happy hours with the children in your care singing these songs and listening to the accompanying recordings at fiddlefoxmusic.com There, you'll also find coloring pages and other printable activities for all the books in our Heritage Songbook Series.

We've also included color-coded sheet music so young instrumentalists can play and sing along. We recommend using colored rainbow bells that match up with our notation system, but you can also use colored stickers on piano keys or ukulele frets if you would like.

Happy Music-Making!

From the Fiddlefox

www.fiddlefoxmusic.com

4

TABLE OF CONTENTS

TURKISH HERITAGE
SONGBOOK

Fiddlefox

MERHABA (HELLO) FROM TURKEY!

UKRAINE

RUSSIA

BULGARIA

BLACK SEA

GEORGIA

Istanbul

ARMENIA

Ankara

TURKEY

IRAN

SYRIA

IRAQ

Turkey is a country larger than the state of Texas that bridges the continents of Europe and Asia. Its capital city is Ankara, but its most famous city is Istanbul. Eight neighboring countries surround Turkey as well as the Mediterranean Sea, the Aegean Sea, and the Black Sea.

People have lived in Turkey for many thousands of years and have seen the rise and fall of the Roman, Byzantine, and Ottoman Empires. Turkey is a true crossroads of culture, mixing customs, artwork, and food from the Middle East, North Africa, Eastern Europe, and ancient Rome. Today, children in Turkey are very much like children in the United States. They love to play soccer, go to school, listen to music, and spend time with their families.

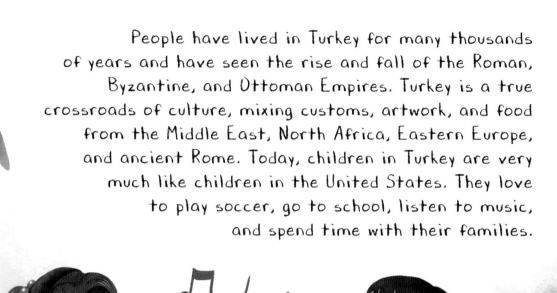

Turkey is famous for many foods including baklava, a flaky pastry layered with honey and nuts, and Turkish Delight or lokum, a jelly-like candy flavored with orange, lemon, or rose water.

Hoş Geldiniz! (Welcome!)

8

YAĞ SATARIM
OIL FOR SALE

Yağ satarim, bal satarim.
Oil for sale, honey for sale.

Ustam öldü, ben satarim.
Master's gone, and I cannot fail.

UPSTAMIN KÜRKÜ SARIDIR,
DRESSED UP IN HIS FINE YELLOW COAT,

SATSAM ONBEŞ LIRADIR.
FIFTEEN LIRA FOR THE LOT.

ZAM-BAK ZUM-BAK
ZAM-BAK ZUM-BAK

DÖN ARKANA IYI BAK!
DROP IT AND YOU WALK WALK!

11

12

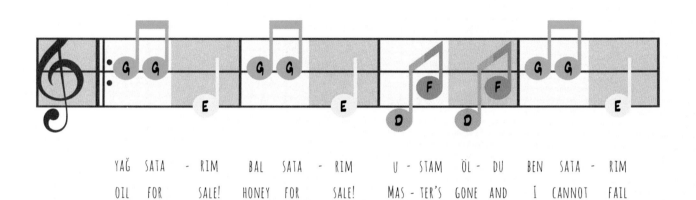

YAĞ SATARIM
OIL FOR SALE

D E F G

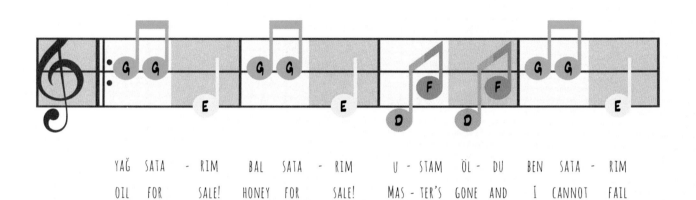

YAĞ SATA - RIM   BAL SATA - RIM   U - STAM ÖL - DU   BEN SATA - RIM
OIL FOR   SALE!   HONEY FOR   SALE!   MAS - TER'S GONE AND   I CANNOT FAIL

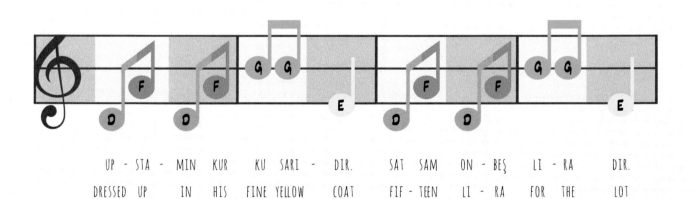

UP - STA - MIN KUR   KU SARI - DIR.   SAT SAM   ON - BEŞ   LI - RA   DIR.
DRESSED UP   IN HIS   FINE YELLOW   COAT   FIF - TEEN   LI - RA   FOR THE   LOT

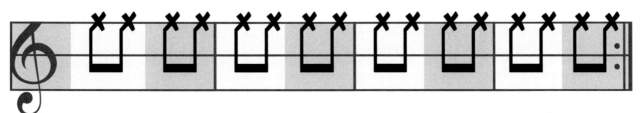

ZAM - BAK   ZUM - BAK   DON AR-KA-NA   IYI   BAK,   ZAM - BAK,   ZUM - BAK,   DON AR-KA-NA   IYI   BAK

DRESSED   UP   IN   HIS   DROP IT AND YOU   WALK   WALK   ZAM - BAK,   ZUM - BAK,   DROP IT AND YOU   WALK   WALK!

Black "x" notes mean play just the rhythm no note.
You can clap, drum, or tap!

MINI MINI BIR KUŞ
ITTY BITTY BIRDIE

MINI MINI BIR KUŞ DONMUŞTU
Itty bitty birdie frozen still

PENCEREME DONMUŞTU
There upon my window sill

Aldım onu içeriye
Take him home inside the heat

16

"Cik cik cik cik" ötsün diye!
So he can sing
"tweet tweet tweet tweet!"

Pir pir ederken canlandi
Itty bitty birdie flew away

Ellerim bak boş kaldi
Come again another day

18

Mini Mini Bir Kuş
Itty Bitty Birdie

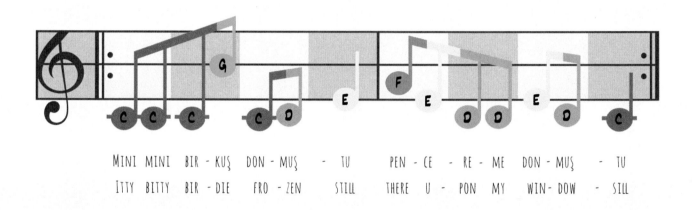

MINI MINI BIR - KUŞ DON - MUŞ - TU   PEN - CE - RE - ME DON - MUŞ - TU
ITTY BITTY BIR - DIE FRO - ZEN STILL   THERE U - PON MY WIN - DOW - SILL

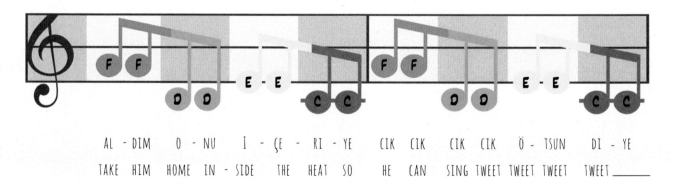

AL - DIM O - NU İ - ÇE - RI - YE   CIK CIK CIK CIK Ö - TSUN DI - YE
TAKE HIM HOME IN - SIDE THE HEAT SO   HE CAN SING TWEET TWEET TWEET TWEET_____

19

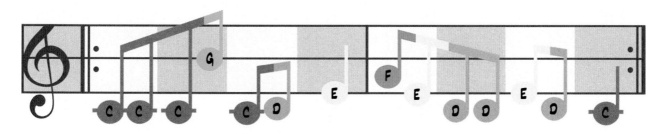

PIR PIR E-DER-KEN CAN-LAN - DI   EL -CE -LERIM BAK BOŞ KAL - DI
ITTY BITTY BIR-DIE FLEW A - WAY   COME A - GAIN A - NO -THER   DAY.

DANDINI DANDINI DASTANA

DANDINI DANDINI DASTANA . . .

21

DANALAR GIRMIŞ BOSTANA!
NOW THE GATE IS OPEN;
COWS IN THE FARM!

22

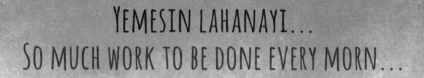

YEMESIN LAHANAYI...
SO MUCH WORK TO BE DONE EVERY MORN...

DANDINI DANDINI DASTANA

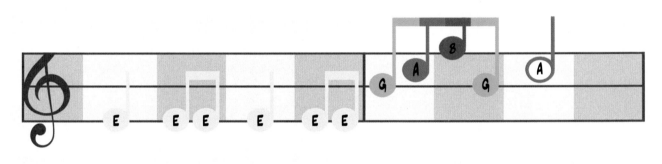

DAN - DI - NI DAN - DI - NI DA - STA - NA

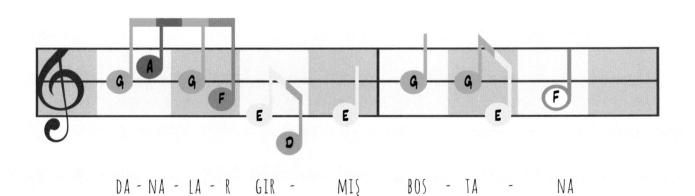

DA - NA - LA - R GIR - MIŞ BOS - TA - NA
NOW THE GATE IS O - PEN! COWS IN THE FARM!

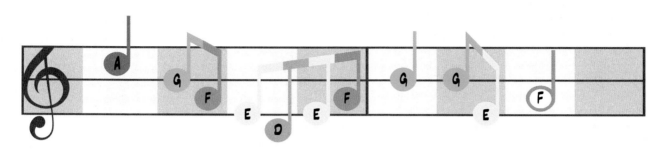

KOV BO - STA - N - CI___ DA - NA - YI!
DON'T EAT THE CA - BA - GES!___ DON'T EAT THE CORN!

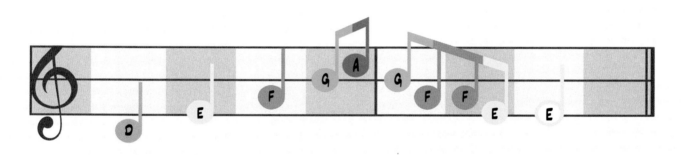

YE ME - SIN LA - HA - NA - YI
SO MUCH WORK TO BE DONE___ EV -'RY MORN!

26

KARGA İLE TILKI
THE CROW AND THE FOX

BIR GÜN BIR HIRSIZ KARGA
ONE FINE DAY A WILY CROW

HA HA HA HA HA HA

BIR PARÇA PEYNIR ÇALMIŞ
STOLE MY CHEESE AS STORIES GO

HA HA HA HA HA

27

KONMUŞ BIR DALDA KALMIŞ
SINGING OUT INTO THE BREEZE

ETRAFI SEYRE DALMIŞ
WITH HIS BEAK STILL FULL OF CHEESE

HA HA HA HA HA HA

HA HA HA HA HA

"ORDAN GEÇEN BIR TILKI?"
"WHO COULD MAKE THAT
LOVELY SOUND?"

ŞEN SESINLE ÖT DEMIŞ
ASKED THE FOX DOWN ON
THE GROUND

HA HA HA HA HA HA

HA HA HA HA HA

29

APTAL KARGA GAK DEMIŞ
CROW OPENED HIS BEAK TO SHOUT

HA HA HA HA HA HA

PEYNIRI TILKI YEMIŞ
AND DROPPED THE CHEESE IN
Fox's MOUTH

HA HA HA HA HA

TURKISH TRADITIONAL

KARGA İLE TILKI
The Crow and the Fox

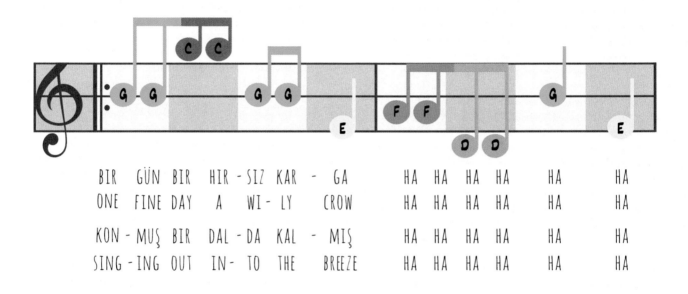

BIR GÜN BIR HIR-SIZ KAR - GA HA HA HA HA HA HA
ONE FINE DAY A WI-LY CROW HA HA HA HA HA HA

KON - MUŞ BIR DAL-DA KAL - MIŞ HA HA HA HA HA HA
SING -ING OUT IN- TO THE BREEZE HA HA HA HA HA HA

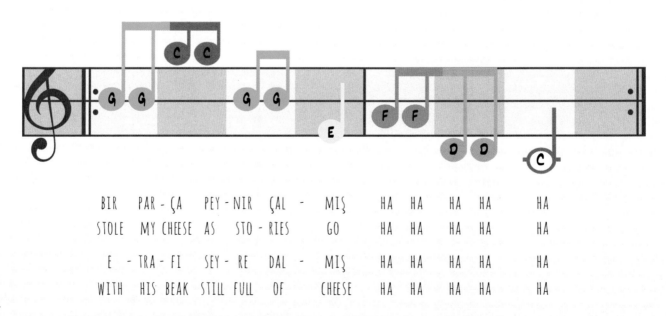

BIR PAR - ÇA PEY-NIR ÇAL - MIŞ HA HA HA HA HA
STOLE MY CHEESE AS STO - RIES GO HA HA HA HA HA

E - TRA-FI SEY- RE DAL - MIŞ HA HA HA HA HA
WITH HIS BEAK STILL FULL OF CHEESE HA HA HA HA HA

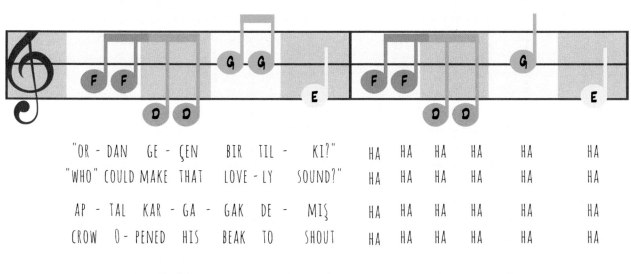

"OR - DAN GE - ÇEN BIR TIL - KI?" HA HA HA HA HA HA
"WHO" COULD MAKE THAT LOVE -LY SOUND?" HA HA HA HA HA HA

AP - TAL KAR - GA - GAK DE - MIŞ HA HA HA HA HA HA
CROW O- PENED HIS BEAK TO SHOUT HA HA HA HA HA HA

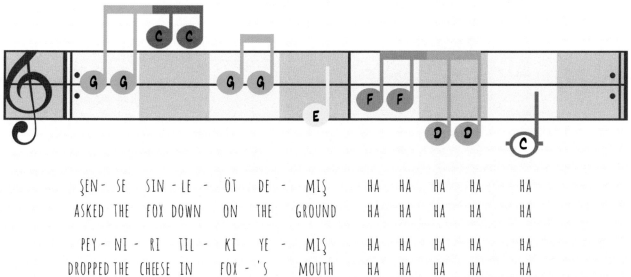

ŞEN- SE SIN -LE - ÖT DE - MIŞ HA HA HA HA HA
ASKED THE FOX DOWN ON THE GROUND HA HA HA HA HA

PEY- NI - RI TIL - KI YE - MIŞ HA HA HA HA HA
DROPPED THE CHEESE IN FOX - 'S MOUTH HA HA HA HA HA

32

BRING A WORLD OF MUSIC HOME WITH
FIDDLEFOX WORLD HERITAGE SONGBOOKS!

Available on iBooks, Amazon and Spotify!
www.fiddlefoxmusic.com

64542040R00022

Made in the USA
Middletown, DE
29 August 2019